Po 01351
5.32

An Austin ambulance of the British Red Cross in 1928. It has clear windows in the saloon, although there were blinds that could be pulled down to ensure some privacy for the patient.

AMBULANCES

Chris Batten

Shire Publications Ltd

CONTENTS

Published in 1996 by Shire Publications Ltd, Cromwell House, Church Street, Princes Risborough, Buckinghamshire HP27 9AA, UK. Copyright © 1996 by Chris Batten. First published 1996. Shire Album 328. ISBN 0 7478 0329 3.
Chris Batten is hereby identified as the author of this work in accordance with Section 77 of the Copyright, Designs and Patents Act 1988.

Printed in Great Britain by CIT Printing Services, Press Buildings, Merlins Bridge, Haverfordwest, Pembrokeshire SA61 1XF.

British Library Cataloguing in Publication Data. Batten, Chris. Ambulances. – (Shire Album; no. 328). 1. Ambulances – Great Britain – History. I. Title. 629.2'2234'0941. ISBN 0-7478-0329-3.

Editorial consultant: Michael E. Ware, Curator of the National Motor Museum, Beaulieu.

ACKNOWLEDGEMENTS
Illustrations are acknowledged as follows: D. Andrews Collection, page 5; Chris Batten, pages 4, 9, 13 (top and centre), 14 (top and centre), 18 (bottom), 19 (both), 22 (top), 24, 28 (both), 29, 31 (bottom), and front cover; British Ambulance Society Archives, pages 1, 7, 8, 10, 11, 12, 13 (bottom), 14 (bottom), 15 (bottom), 16, 17, 18 (top), 20, 22 (bottom), 25 (bottom), 27 (bottom); City of Birmingham Ambulance Service, via British Ambulance Society, page 25 (top); S. Greenaway, pages 30, 31 (top and centre), 32 (both); Charles Keevil, via British Ambulance Society, page 23 (both); Roger Leonard, pages 2, 26, 27 (top); NSW Health, page 6 (top); A. Saunderson, page 15 (top).

Cover: *A Morris Commercial ambulance of the 1930s, with bodywork believed to be by Stewart & Arden. This vehicle served in Middlesex but has been preserved in the green livery of the Portsmouth Voluntary Ambulance Service.*

A Bedford J1/Lomas ambulance, registration UXE 150G, supplied to Luton Ambulance Service in 1969. The service was incorporated into Bedfordshire Ambulance Service in the 1974 reorganisation, and later combined with Hertfordshire to form Bedfordshire and Hertfordshire Ambulance Service.

Above: *A Ford Transit ambulance of the Hampshire Ambulance Service. Note that the badge shown is the county badge which was used before the introduction of the crown badge in the 1980s.*

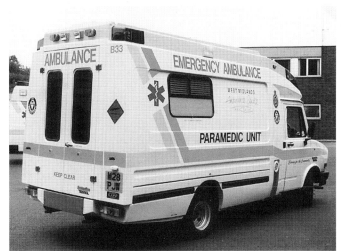

Left and below: *Colourful paramedic liveries started to appear in the late 1980s. These examples are Leyland DAFs of West Midlands Ambulance Service.*

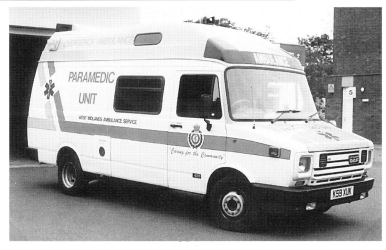

FURTHER READING

There have been very few books on ambulances. The only one which is still available is:
Geary, L. *Ambulances*. Ian Henry Publications, 1984.

References to the history and development of ambulances and the ambulance service can be found in the following books:

Chapman, Paul, and Mills, Jeremy. *Paramedics*. BBC Publications, 1994. The book of the television series.

Cole-Mackintosh, Ronnie. *A Century of Service to Mankind*. Century Banham, 1986. The story of St John Ambulance.

Hambley, John A.S. *London Transport Buses and Coaches 1939-1945*. Images, 1995.

Kernaghan, Pam. *St John Ambulance in World War II*. Museum and Library of the Order of St John, 1995.

Kirkland, Jack. *Blue Lights and Bandages*. Seanachaidh, 1989. Thirty-six years with the Scottish Ambulance Service.

Lees, Steve, and McGregor, Peter. *Ninety Years of Ambulances in and around Nottingham*. Nottingham Ambulance Historical Research, 1993.

Samuelson, Pauline. *I Owe My Life*. Bloomsbury, 1995. Celebrating 125 years of the Red Cross.

Spears, Robert. *Patients Are People*. Noel Richardson, 1994. An account of Salford Ambulance Service.

Taylor, James, and Morrison, Bob. *Modern Military Land-Rovers in Colour 1971-1994*. Windrow & Greene, 1994.

Wood, Emily. *The Red Cross Story*. Dorling Kindersley, 1995.

BRITISH AMBULANCE SOCIETY

The British Ambulance Society is devoted to preserving ambulances and recording their history. It publishes a regular newsletter and magazine, *Ambulance Scene*. Anyone interested should write to the British Ambulance Society, 21 Victoria Road, Horley, Surrey RH6 9BN.

PLACES TO VISIT

At present there is no museum open to the public devoted to ambulances. Examples of Second World War ambulances can be seen at the Imperial War Museum site at Duxford Airfield, Duxford, Cambridge CB2 4QR (telephone: 01223 835000).

The British Ambulance Society organises an annual National Emergency Vehicles Show, which features ambulances, including preserved examples pictured in this Album.

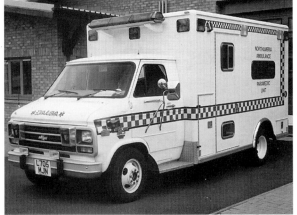

Some services looked abroad for vehicles. The American influence is shown by a Chevrolet ambulance built in the USA, in service with Northumbria Ambulance Service in 1993.

The first ambulance, Baron Larrey's 'ambulance volante' of 1792, a two-horse flying ambulance with space for two patients.

EARLY AMBULANCES

The dictionary defines an ambulance as 'a conveyance for the sick or wounded; a mobile field hospital'. It is astonishing that as recently as the end of the nineteenth century there were hardly any ambulances and the sick and injured were expected to get to hospital in any way they could.

The development of the ambulance in the twentieth century has been mainly due to the efforts of specialist coachbuilders and bodybuilders; motor manufacturers generally provided only the chassis. As first-aid treatment and the skills of ambulance crews have improved, especially over the last few years, the ambulance has changed from being a simple carrier of a patient to become a rapid-response unit designed to meet the needs of a casualty at the scene of an accident or in cases of sudden illness.

THE FIRST AMBULANCES

Transporting the wounded from the battlefield was always a problem. Teams of strong men followed Roman centurions into battle to pick up the injured and administer first aid, encouraged by incentive payments for each life saved.

Until the end of the eighteenth century horses, carts, hammocks, coaches and even sedan chairs were all used to carry the sick and injured. However, it was not until the Napoleonic Wars that the first use of the term 'ambulance' can be traced. It was a French army surgeon, Baron Jean Dominique Larrey (1766-1842), who in 1792 introduced what he called *ambulances volantes*. Larrey often took these 'flying ambulances' into the thick of battle. There were two types: light, covered two-wheeled vehicles with space for two patients, drawn by two horses for rapid transport over flat firm ground; and a heavier, four-wheeled version accommodating two or four patients, drawn by four horses, for use over rough or heavy terrain. The ambulances were fitted with removable litters and carried food, water, bandages and other medical equipment. Larrey used these as mobile treatment units, often carrying out surgery, including amputations, in the field. The use of ambulances and the number of lives saved as a result that would otherwise have been lost caused much comment and the use of such vehicles was quickly adopted by other armies. Baron Larrey appreciated the importance not only of careful transportation of the injured but also the need to treat them promptly at the scene before moving them – a facility that is only now being provided generally with paramedic units some 150 years later.

Baron Larrey went on to develop and design various types of ambulance to suit the varying conditions his armies met, including mule litters and camel litters for use by the French serving in Africa. Another French Army surgeon, Baron Percy, devised a procedure for training in litter handling and stretcher bearing.

In the 1850s a Regulation Pattern British Miliary Ambulance was introduced, designed by a committee at the Royal Carriage Department, Woolwich. The result was not a great success and it received unfavourable reports when it was used in the Crimea. However, the British ambulance wagon continued for over fifty years and saw considerable service during the Boer Wars.

CIVILIAN AMBULANCES FOR INFECTIOUS PATIENTS

The ambulance was seen very much as a military item. The civilian population had managed without them before the wars of the early nineteenth century, getting to hospital by whatever means they could.

The need to provide a general ambulance service at public expense was not recognised until the great cholera epidemic of 1832, when it became necessary to move large numbers of patients with infectious diseases such as cholera and smallpox. Under the 1866 Sanitary Act conveyances were provided to take infectious patients to special isolation hospitals and the Local Government Board arranged for the provision of suitable ambulances, which were little more than four-wheeled horse-drawn vans. However, the stigma attached to the 'fever ambulances' was such that patients refused to travel in them. This became so widespread that vehicles had to be built to resemble ordinary carriages but with an opening at the back to allow stretchers to slide in.

The brougham was a widely used and neat all-weather four-wheeler which was modified for use as an ambulance by fitting a door at the rear for a stretcher to enter. Atkinson & Philipson, coachbuilders of Newcastle upon Tyne from 1794, built ambulances from 1876, supplying the Metropolitan Asylums Board with a brougham ambulance in 1888. The basic price was £87, with a sliding stretcher as an extra. A similar vehicle was advertised by Holmes & Company of Der-

A Metropolitan Asylums Board horse ambulance of c.1880, used to convey fever patients to isolation hospital. There was space for two patients and a seat for an attendant. The livery was dark green. This example is now preserved by the London Ambulance Service.

A horse-drawn ambulance used by the City of Bradford c.1906 with a body built by Wilson & Stockall, coachbuilders of Bury, Lancashire. It cost £135 and was housed at the fire station. The crew comprised a fireman driver and a policeman attendant.

by at the turn of the century for £80. The Metropolitan Asylums Board was responsible for dealing with infectious cases in London, many of whom were transported to fever ships moored in the Thames off Dartford.

GENERAL CIVILIAN AMBULANCES

Accidents and cases of sudden illness were still usually dealt with by the local police, who transported patients to hospital, or by a doctor, who might commandeer a passing horse vehicle or use a hand litter. The police were not specially trained for this role and many thought it not to be part of their job.

Civilian ambulances for patients such as accident victims were first provided in 1882 with the formation of the London Horse Ambulance Service under the presidency of the Duke of Cambridge. This did not prove a success and the service soon came to an end because it was not advertised and local hospitals refused to adopt the scheme, deeming the charge of between five and ten shillings each time they hired an ambulance to be too high.

It was the St John Ambulance Brigade, formed in 1887, that provided the first regular civilian ambulance service for non-infectious cases in Great Britain, starting with a horse ambulance.

THE AMBULANCE LITTER

Most litters had two wheels on a single axle with a stretcher that could be lifted on to the frame and secured. Other designs had two extra, centrally positioned small wheels, one in front of and one behind the axle, to prevent the litter from tipping. Most were of light construction with pram-type wire-spoked wheels.

The first use of hand litters was by the Prussians in a war with Denmark in 1864. In 1889 H. L. Bischoffscheim founded the Hospitals Association Street Ambulance Service. At his own expense Bischoffscheim provided sixty-two wheeled litters to operate from police stations, fire stations and cab ranks. The litters and other first-aid equipment were kept in weatherproof sheds and the practice spread throughout Britain. Policemen and cab drivers acted as attendants. By

Ambulance litters were used extensively at the end of the nineteenth century, not only in the United Kingdom. This example was used in Sydney, Australia, in 1895.

1909 the police had some four hundred wheeled litters, one of which has been preserved by the Metropolitan Police Museum.

There were several manufacturers, with the cost of a hand litter in 1910 being about £12. One used by the Lancashire Fire Brigade was described as a 'Useful First Aid, Fire and Ambulance Carriage'. This carried hose and hydrant fittings as well as being convertible into a full-length ambulance litter.

BICYCLE AMBULANCES

Outside London the St John Ambulance Brigade was developing its services. These included fixing a stretcher between two bicycles and the formation in 1892 of the Cycling Division of St John Ambulance,

An advertisement for an ambulance litter by Simmons & Company of Bermondsey c.1910. This firm supplied litters to Marylebone Corporation, Plymouth Police, the London County Council, the Metropolitan Asylums Board and London Electric Tramways.

A twin tandem cycle ambulance c.1904 with connected steering and a weatherproof litter of the St John Ambulance Brigade. Motorcycle combination ambulances were also developed and used during the First World War.

Leicester. As cycles required a minimum of maintenance, were easy to store and could be ridden by most able-bodied people, a variety of bicycle ambulances followed. A quadricycle ambulance was designed in 1895 by Alldays & Onions of Birmingham, who later supplied new motor ambulances to the War Office in the First World War. An unusual bicycle capable of simple conversion into a hand litter was introduced in 1906, intended for use by country policemen on patrol. The officers of the 5th (West Middlesex) Volunteer Rifle Corps designed their own bicycle ambulance in 1907. In the same year the Patent Cycle Ambulance Company of Sloane Street, Manchester, offered several machines. A single tandem ambulance was marketed by the Tandem Tricycle Ambulance Company of Manchester in 1909 at a cost of £35. The twin ambulance powered by four cyclists proved to be a fast machine over short distances and a useful means of ambulance transport for a longer journey.

By 1900 there were numerous ambulance services throughout Britain. They started to appear at mines and other industrial sites, usually with staff trained by the St John Ambulance Association. Some

hospitals had ambulances, although many belonged to, and were staffed by, the local police force. In Scotland the St Andrew's Ambulance Association in Glasgow had an ambulance wagon provided at public subscription. St John Ambulance also formed an Invalid Transport Corps to take the poor and needy to and from hospital.

MOTOR AMBULANCES

The horseless carriage was quickly seen by the various ambulance services as a means of improving ambulance transport. A Thorneycroft steam ambulance, capable of carrying eight patients at 5 mph (8 km/h), was trialled by the Metropolitan Asylums Board in 1903, but because it was slow and gave a rough ride it was soon withdrawn. This vehicle was mainly used to carry patients to the MAB's ferry boats which carried patients down the Thames to the Dartford hospital complex. So large was the Dartford site that a tramway was constructed to facilitate movement of patients. Both ferries and ambulance trams continued in service until 1930. The first motor ambulance used by the MAB was introduced in 1905, and by 1908 the Board had a fleet of seven Dennis

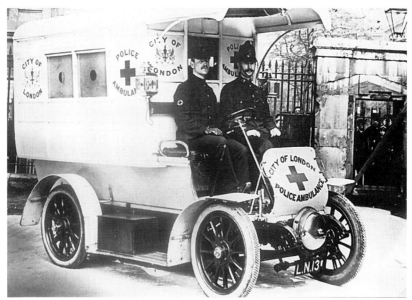

The 1907 Electromobile electric ambulance of the City of London Police.

ambulances supplemented by a single-deck bus for up to sixteen convalescent patients.

Thus various organisations were providing ambulance services and a variety of vehicles was used, all based on commercial car or van chassis. Bodies were constructed by local coachbuilders, who used many ingenious methods to provide access for patients. Some vehicles used standard bodies; for example, Dennis offered a vehicle closely resembling a contemporary taxicab with the stretcher loaded from the rear through the boot. The patient's legs rested in the space beside the driver, where, in the taxi version, the luggage was stowed.

ELECTRIC AMBULANCES

On 13th May 1907 the City of London Police introduced an emergency ambulance service using an electric ambulance made by the Electromobile Company and allocated for use at St Bartholomew's Hospital. It was registered LN13, with a chassis by Greenwood & Batley of Leeds and a body to a design of the St John Ambulance Brigade. It could be called from any of the force's fifty-seven telephone posts throughout the City. The electric ambulance dealt with 120-130 cases per month. After six months the average time taken for the ambulance to arrive at an accident was under four minutes and the time to convey the patient to hospital about nine minutes, half the time taken by a horse-drawn ambulance.

In 1909 another Electromobile ambulance was stationed at New Street, Bishopsgate. So successful was the service that a third electric ambulance, this time built by Cedes, was purchased in 1916. During the First World War the ambulances were placed, when available, at the disposal of the City of London Branch of the British Red Cross Society to convey sick and wounded troops who had arrived by train from London rail termini to hospitals. In 1927 they were replaced by three Crossley petrol-engined ambulances.

From 1912 the Port of London Authority Police Ambulance Service operated similar electric ambulances based at the London, West India, Surrey Commercial, Victoria and Albert docks. These, too, were later replaced by motor ambulances.

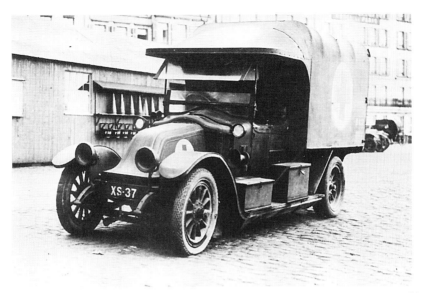

A Renault ambulance built and used during the First World War. This example was operated by the Red Cross at Boulogne in 1916 and was probably converted from a car.

THE FIRST WORLD WAR

Before the First World War (1914-18) the Army Service Corps (later Royal Army Service Corps) operated a few 'motor ambulance vans'. The first, a Straker-Squire, was introduced in 1908, and a Wolseley Siddeley in 1910. Both of these had simple wooden bodies. In 1914 the St John Ambulance and the British Red Cross joined together and began to arrange the conversion into motor ambulances of a collection of cars donated by the public. By October 1914 there were already 120 ambulances in France.

The mainstay of the army was still the horse-drawn wagon but many motor vehicles were adapted for use to meet the ever growing number of casualties. Heavy ambulances, staffed by a driver and one attendant, carried four stretchers or eight sitting cases and were used to transport wounded men from forward-area dressing stations to hospitals or hospital trains, and between hospitals. Examples were the Siddeley-Deasy, of which over 500 saw service, and the Sunbeam, which was produced by Rover and became the standard army heavy ambulance. By 1918 over 1600 were in service. War Department require-

ments included a central passage, interior lining, dual rear wheels, ventilators and the Red Cross special heating system. Other popular makes included Austin, Clement-Talbot, Crossley, Daimler, Ford, Maxwell, Napier, Star, Sunbeam, Vauxhall and Wolseley, as well as American Buicks, Fords and GMCs.

Light ambulances carried crew plus four sitting or two stretcher cases and were used where the terrain was bad. The usual type was the Ford Model 'T'. Although a pacifist, Henry Ford provided hundreds of Model 'T' chassis specifically for use as vehicles to transport the wounded and sick. Until 1915 they were produced by Ford Canada and shipped to Europe but in that year production was transferred to the Ford factory in Manchester. 2645 Ford ambulances were produced between 1915 and the end of the war. The Model 'T' comprised a basic chassis with bulkhead and bonnet and was supplied with a wide variety of bodies ranging from a simple tent-like covering on a flat bed through canvas-covered vans to custom-built ambulance bodies. The transverse semi-elliptical springs for the suspension gave a

Two Rover ambulances, with registration numbers S 1050 and DUR 54, built during the First World War for service with the Royal Navy. The livery appears to be grey.

good ride for the patient. The four-cylinder petrol engine of 2.85 litres was rated at 20 horsepower. The wheelbase was 100 inches (2.5 metres) and had a two-speed encyclic transmission. Because the wheelbase was short, there was a considerable amount of rear overhang which could not be modified sufficiently to accept the standard British Army stretcher. To overcome the problem, four holes were drilled in the tailboard of the vehicles and canvas bags fixed over the holes to allow the ends of the stretchers to poke through. The canvas bags prevented cold air entering the ambulance interior. British doctors at the front pronounced the Model 'T' the fittest for ambulance work.

The Royal Flying Corps used the Crossley 20/25 horsepower 15 cwt (750 kg) truck as their standard tender during the war and many of these were used as ambulances. The engine was four-cylinder petrol of 4.54 litres rated at 25 horsepower with a wheelbase of 126 inches (4.1 metres) and a four-speed crash gearbox. Many of the Crossleys were used

after the war by local ambulance services, which fitted new custom-built bodies.

THE AMBULANCE COLUMN

The Ambulance Column was a band of volunteers who provided transport from stations to hospitals for troops returning on ambulance trains. The fleet of vehicles grew as sponsorship was given by many institutions. The Baltic Exchange provided Rolls-Royce ambulances, and other fine ambulances were provided and operated by staff from the Stock Exchange. At one time more than seventy were available, including Daimlers, Lanchesters, Wolseleys and Sunbeams, as well as private cars to take the walking wounded. In many cases the vehicles were driven and maintained by their owners.

On 22nd March 1916 the Column paraded at Buckingham Palace for inspection by King George V and in June 1918 the King and Queen were present to watch detraining at Waterloo station. Eventually the task was finished and the Ambulance Column disbanded in February 1919, hav-

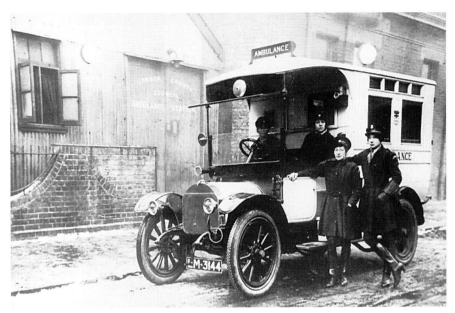

During the First World War women took on many new roles, including driving ambulances and attending patients. This London County Council ambulance crew is pictured outside an ambulance station.

ing transported over 600,000 cases. Many of the ambulances used by the Column were painted grey with a red cross and the name of the institution responsible for the vehicle.

MILITARY LIVERIES

Under the Geneva Convention it was agreed that ambulances would not carry weapons or materials of war and that medical personnel would not be issued with any firearms. Therefore, to avoid being attacked by the enemy, ambulances carried prominent red crosses. For British ambulances the red cross was carried in a white circle. The ambulances were mainly khaki in colour, although the canvas bodies on some of the more basic versions varied. Ambulances provided jointly by the St John Ambulance service and the British Red Cross carried a small red cross in a white circle but with 'Order of St John' and 'British Red Cross Society' either side of this. The red cross was not always respected and there were a number of reports – mainly used for propaganda purposes – of ambulances not carrying red crosses because of this. The red cross was also applied to other non-combat vehicles such as mobile kitchens and workshops, but after the war the International Committee revised its convention to make clear that the use of the red cross should be confined to vehicles carrying casualties and engaged in the saving of life.

WOMEN CREWS

Although women had cared for sick and wounded soldiers since before Florence Nightingale went to the Crimea in 1854, the First World War provided the first opportunities for them to crew ambulances when the lack of able-bodied men forced a number of the civilian ambulance services to introduce female crews. The London County Council (LCC), for example, had a number of women drivers and attendants, who, by showing themselves capable of doing the job, started the tradition of women ambulance personnel.

A Home Ambulance Service Ford 'T' (1922) used at Uckfield, East Sussex. The livery was black.

THE INTER-WAR YEARS

THE HOME AMBULANCE SERVICE

After the war the Order of St John and the British Red Cross Society continued to work together to meet the peacetime ambulance requirements, forming the Home Ambulance Committee. In 1919 all ambulances considered serviceable were returned to the United Kingdom, reconditioned and made ready for civilian use by the Red Cross at its own workshops.

Ambulance stations were provided throughout Britain on what was intended to be a trial basis. However, it quickly became apparent that a general ambulance service for the civilian population was needed. The Home Ambulance Service was thus the beginning of a national ambulance service.

Its ambulances were originally painted black with the same joint insignia that had been used during the war, usually carried around a red cross in a white circle. Where the service was primarily provided by the St John Ambulance, the badges of both organisations were sometimes shown in the white circle. The vehicles carried the title HOME AMBULANCE SERVICE in white lettering.

So successful was the service that it continued until after the Second World War and well into the years of a true National Health Service. After 1945 the livery for Red Cross vehicles changed to dark blue. Apart from the Home Ambulance Service, ambulance facilities were also provided by local authorities, the police, fire brigade and other voluntary organisations.

VEHICLES

In the 1920s more manufacturers were providing ambulances. Vauxhall, Ford, Morris, Austin, Dennis and Bedford all offered chassis which could be mounted with an ambulance body. Some specialists producing complete ambulances entered the market, such as W. & G. Du Cros, who provided ambulances to the Metropolitan Asylums Board, and Talbot, who provided vehicles to a large number of users, including the LCC, Kent Health Authority, the Army and the Royal Navy.

Bodies were built by a wide variety of coachbuilders, some of whom, such as Wadhams, continued to build ambulances for many years. Many coachbuilders built one-off bodies for local use as there was often only one ambulance stationed in a particular area and it was replaced only occasionally. There were big variations between adapted vans and sophisticated custom-built ambulances.

Liveries varied, with black, grey, blue, green and maroon being used. White was little used, except in London by the LCC.

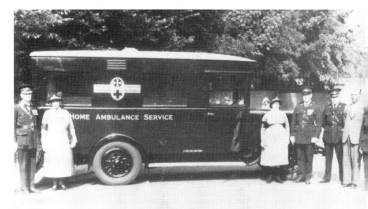

An unidentified make of ambulance of the Home Ambulance Service c.1930. It displays the joint Red Cross and St John Ambulance insignia rather than the usual red cross. The body was probably built by a local coachbuilder.

Austin and Morris ambulances at Addiscombe Motor Ambulance Service base, Croydon. The crew members appear to have been St John Ambulance personnel.

A Morris Commercial ambulance with a Lomas body operated by Farnborough Urban District Council, Hampshire, in 1930-1, and pictured in the town-hall yard. The vehicle had only rear brakes with a bell-push positioned between the driver's legs.

An ambulance of the Metropolitan Asylums Board purpose-built by W. & G. Du Cros in 1927. The livery is two-tone grey. The chassis was specially designed for ambulance work jointly by the MAB and the maker. The vehicle is now preserved by the London Ambulance Service.

A Talbot ambulance, built by Clement Talbot at their factory in Barlby Road, Kensington, pictured outside Sidcup fire station, Kent, in the 1930s. These ambulances were produced from 1920 to 1938, by which time the business had been acquired by the Rootes Group.

A Dennis Arrow coach used by the London County Council to take infectious patients to isolation hospital at Dartford. It replaced the service provided by the Metropolitan Asylums Board. The coach could carry six stretcher patients, three on each side. In addition to a large hinged door at the rear, it had sliding doors on both sides.

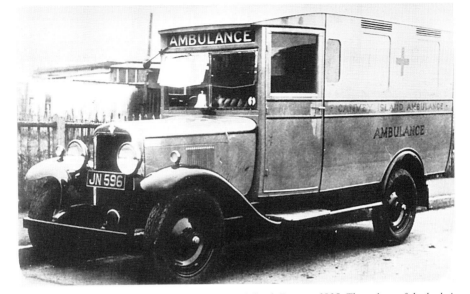

A Morris Commercial ambulance used in Canvey Island, Essex, c.1935. The colour of the body is not known but it may have been grey. Apart from the LCC fleet, few ambulances were white before the 1950s and 1960s.

Gloucester City Fire Brigade Vauxhall ambulance c.1936. Many areas relied on the local fire brigade or police for emergency cover. The livery appears to be all black.

Organisation and standards of service still tended to be somewhat haphazard. Many crews, especially those employed by local authorities, were still engaged purely as drivers and the standard of first-aid training was limited. The aim was simply to get the casualty to hospital, where treatment could take place.

THE SECOND WORLD WAR

CIVILIAN AMBULANCES

At the outbreak of the Second World War large numbers of coaches and buses were commandeered primarily to evacuate hospital patients and to stand by in case of major attacks on cities. The Phoney War of late 1939 and early 1940 gave the authorities time to order custom-built ambulances. The unco-ordinated ambulance services and their assortment of vehicles did not meet existing demands, let alone wartime needs. Indeed, the first months of the blackout resulted in a dramatic increase in the numbers of road casualties.

The commandeered coaches were returned for regular bus services, not least to get war workers to work. All the main vehicle manufacturers were fully occupied producing aircraft, munitions and military vehicles, so to cover the immediate need all manner of vans and lorries were designated as ambulances, usually overnight, returning to their commercial role by day. Many private cars, off the road because their owners or drivers were in the forces or because of a shortage of petrol, had the rear section replaced with a standard-size basic ambulance body. Cars selected were normally 20 horsepower or more with a 9 foot 6 inch (2.9 metre) wheelbase and included the Austin 20, Vauxhall 20 and Morris 20, as well as various Humbers, Daimlers and American Packards and Buicks.

In view of their fate, the large numbers handed over is surprising, with others coming from local councils or breakers' yards in the south of England. Many conversions were undertaken by Park Ward Ltd, coachbuilders of London, and the completed ambulances were distributed to Air Raid Precautions (ARP) groups throughout Britain. The bodies were box-shaped and many were of wooden tongued and grooved construction. The roof was

Women ambulance crews maintaining a Hampshire County Council ambulance converted from a car for war work in the Second World War.

A London Auxiliary Ambulance Service ambulance converted from a car. It is very basic with no rear doors. Note the 'AA' number on the side. Many large sedans such as Buicks were converted at the LCC Wandsworth depot.

generally made of stretched canvas and the rear simply had two canvas curtains. Most bodies had room for four stretchers in two banks of two.

The Midland ARP service, which was under the control of Lord Dudley, needed six hundred ambulances and he asked the local Wolseley company to design an ambulance body suitable for fitting on to the chassis of a private car. A works car was used as a prototype and a utility body constructed and fitted. Wolseley undertook to purchase and convert six hundred second-hand cars of various makes. Including modifications to the suspension and overhaul of the brakes and lighting system the average cost per vehicle was £50. Notable work was done by these vehicles particularly in Birmingham and Coventry.

Smaller cars were often used to carry stretcher parties. With metal stretchers lashed to the roof, they were used by the ARP as rapid-response units to provide immediate first aid and care.

Vans were also commandeered and used as ambulances. The local volunteer services as well as numerous works ambulances supported as required.

Because of the special position and vulnerability of London the London Auxiliary Ambulance Service was introduced based on the existing regular service. Lon-

don converted many private cars to ambulances and in addition produced large numbers of Bedford 10-12 cwt (500-600 kg) van ambulances at their own LCC workshops from 1940. These had wooden-slatted bodies and were initially painted grey although later vehicles were turned out in standard LCC white. The Auxiliary vehicles could be distinguished from the regular LCC service models as they did not carry the LCC shield on the side and the fleet numbers were prefixed by 'AA'. In London alone 48,709 casualties were removed to hospitals or first-aid posts during the war.

There was no standardised livery for ARP ambulances. Vehicles were generally finished in a flat grey primer. Most in the south of England were austerely lettered 'AMBULANCE' in white and 'ARP', with in some cases an ARP badge. Some Midlands vehicles had red crosses although the use of these was supposedly restricted to military and British Red Cross vehicles. Others carried a large 'A' in a circle on the side. As most saloon cars were originally black, the cabs of some conversions remained this colour and some bodies constructed on them were painted black to match. An example of a black ARP ambulance was operated in Croydon. Some light cars were used to pull

trailers which carried one or two stretchers. Their livery was usually grey or black.

Ambulances had to have restricted headlights in compliance with the blackout regulations; this made the drivers' job much more difficult and there were several instances of ambulances driving into bomb craters. However, the offside headlight of ambulances usually had an illuminated 'A' showing to identify it as an emergency vehicle. Most had no audible or visible means of warning.

MILITARY AMBULANCES

Albion, Austin, Bedford, Ford, Fordson, Humber and Morris provided chassis for military ambulances and the bodies came from a variety of builders. Some saw service in other medical guises, such as mobile dentist, mobile clinic and X-ray units. From across the Atlantic came Dodge and Chevrolet ambulances, which were used by British and allied forces as well as the Americans.

However, the classic and most common ambulance used by the British armed forces was the famous Austin K2. Over thirteen thousand of these were made at Austin's Longbridge works, where production was continuous from 1940 until the war ended. The same type of body, usu-

An Austin K2 with Mann Egerton bodywork and the correct white circle around the red cross. The 'Katy' was the standard Allied ambulance.

A Dodge WC54, the standard United States Army ambulance of the Second World War. This example is now preserved.

ally made by Mann Egerton, was also fitted on Bedford and Morris Commercial chassis, but in far fewer numbers. The 2 ton K2 had an Austin six-cylinder petrol engine. Some went to France, Norway and Russia. The United States forces also had an allocation. Most Austin K2s were in standard olive green or khaki, including those used by the RAF. The British forces' marking was a red cross in a white circle. Red crosses in white squares have been applied to some preserved examples, ambulances used in films and models, perhaps because of the square-sided bodies, but Britain did not adopt this until NATO markings were standardised in the 1950s. The red cross was carried under the terms of the Geneva Convention, which laid down that ambulances would not carry weapons or materials of war. The drivers of most of the British K2s were not medical staff and thus were expected to carry a rifle. Indeed, in the cabs of at least one version there are brackets to take two rifles – which would appear to contravene the Geneva Convention!

The K2 proved extremely reliable in service and many were converted into civil and industrial ambulances after the war. The reliability of the vehicle prompted the war film *Ice Cold in Alex*. It was a K2, numbered A1212251, that Princess Elizabeth, now the Queen, learnt to drive while serving in the ATS at No. 1 MT Centre.

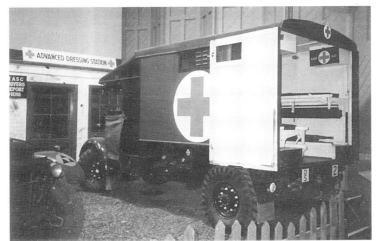

An Austin K2 ambulance.

POST-WAR DEVELOPMENTS

Because of post-war shortages many ambulance services had to continue using wartime utilitarian conversions. The Home Ambulance Service supplemented local services and had over a thousand ambulances available stationed throughout the British Isles. The responsibility for running these vehicles was mainly undertaken by voluntary workers. To build up the fleet, a large-scale conversion of ex-military ambulances, mainly K2s, in good condition, with less than 4000 miles (6437 km) on the clock, was introduced. The Home Ambulance Service's own repair works at Lots Road, Chelsea, carried out most of the general chassis renovation, whilst bodywork conversions were undertaken by a number of companies. Other vehicles in the fleet were based on the Commercial Austin and Bedford. The livery was dark blue with black wings and chassis. One of their first duties was to replace the coaches taking expectant mothers to outlying maternity hospitals.

Great changes followed the Labour victory in the 1945 election and the introduction of the National Heath Service. Section 27 of the National Health Act 1946, effective from 5th July 1948, placed a responsibility on local authorities for the first time to provide a comprehensive ambulance service in their area. How they did it was up to the county and county borough councils, but they found themselves in a difficult and curious situation: they were responsible for organising the service and shared the cost equally with the Exchequer, but they had little or no control over its use. The calls arose because of emergencies and came from hospitals and general practitioners. A further complication was that the catchment areas of hospitals were not related to local authority boundaries. The result was a widely contrasting response from authorities. Some set up their own independent ambulance services whilst others, such as Birmingham, Wolverhampton and Dudley, established joint 'fire and ambulance' services. A clause in the 1946 Act enabled local authorities to co-operate with the voluntary services and a number of close links were forged, examples being Eastbourne, Hastings, Kingston upon Thames and Norfolk.

Where authorities provided their own

A Morris Commercial ambulance of Middlesex County Council showing the type converted from Auxiliary Fire Service heavy pumps after the Second World War to meet vehicle shortages.

ambulances, these were often regarded as part of the municipal transport fleet. In Salford, Lancashire, for instance, the service came under the transport department and the vehicles were the same green as Salford City Transport buses; the original uniforms for the crew were actually bus inspectors' uniforms. The vehicles were taken over from local hospitals, the police ambulance service and a local corporation service provided on behalf of the Health Department of Lancashire County Council. When in 1951 the council invited tenders for a long-distance ambulance, it was not surprising that the Daimler DC27 with bodywork by Barker was chosen as Salford had a number of Daimler buses with the same automatic transmission and was well pleased with them. The inherited vehicles were replaced by Morris Commercial ambulances.

The ambulance crew usually consisted of a driver and an attendant. Normally the only qualifications required were a driving licence and a basic knowledge of first aid. The idea that ambulance crews were merely drivers lasted a long time and this made it difficult for ambulance personnel to achieve recognition for their professionalism.

While it remained difficult to replace vehicles a number of ambulance body-builders and coachbuilders recognised that there was a potentially large market. As commercial chassis became available in 1950, firms such as Lomas, Wadhams, Appleyard and Pilchers manufactured ambulances using chassis such as the Austin K2, Morris Commercial LD1 and Austin Princess. Austin also offered the Austin Welfarer as an ambulance development of their Wayfarer van.

AMBULANCE FROM A FIRE ENGINE

To overcome the immediate shortage of vehicles, some innovative plans were implemented in 1948. For example, Middlesex County Council purchased sixty-two Morris Commercial Auxiliary Fire Service (AFS) heavy pump units in October 1947. Of these fifty-one were rebodied as front-line emergency ambulances, six were converted to ambulance coaches and four were broken up for spares. The conversions were relatively cheap, with new ambulance bodies costing around £750 per conversion.

The bodies were produced by J. S. Keen & Company of Hackney and Stewert & Arden. The chassis were renovated by a number of firms, including Hampshire Car Bodies (HCB), at an average cost of £460 per chassis. So successful was this emergency measure that when new chassis did become available Middlesex County Council supplied them with a similar type of body and the type remained in service until 1964. Several of these vehicles were transferred to the County Civil Defence pool and were retained until 1965.

The livery of the Middlesex vehicles was pale cream with black wings and lining. The Civil Defence machines were repainted in overall dull olive green, the only relief being white lettering with the colourful Civil Defence badge.

OPERATION

The National Heath Act 1946 did not specify any common standard of service provision. By 1953 Cumberland still had no full-time administration or operational ambulance staff. The emphasis was on running a service that was as economical as possible. The Cumberland fleet in 1953 consisted of seven Humber Pullmans, two Daimler DC27s, one Morris Commercial, two Austin Welfarers and an Austin 2 ton chassis with a Wadhams body. Two new Morris Commercials were fitted out to comply with Cumberland's own specification for ambulances to be capable of carrying both lying and sitting patients. Unusually, Cumberland also used wheeled stretchers and where wheeling was possible one man could move a patient. In remote areas agency agreements with voluntary bodies were maintained. Here Cumberland replaced locally purchased vehicles. The local driver was usually a shopkeeper or someone else who could be readily contacted by telephone. Such drivers were paid an annual retainer in return for being ready to turn out at any time. Despite the dependence on part-time help, Cumberland claimed that an ambu-

A Morris Commercial ambulance preserved in the Morris Commercial livery of cream with rust-brown wings and lining.

lance could be at any required place in the county within twenty minutes of an emergency call being received. This took no account of the standard of medical treatment and first aid that would be available for the patient; it typified the view, prevalent until comparatively recently, that the main role of the ambulance service in Britain was to collect patients and convey them to hospital.

Birmingham City Council faced very different problems. Before 1948 there were four ambulance providers: the police dealt with all street accidents; the Public Health Department handled all infectious diseases, tuberculosis and mental patients; there was a voluntary hospital car service run by the Red Cross; but most work was carried out by the Birmingham Hospital Contributory Association. The City Council decided to take direct operational responsibility for a service but entrusted the day-to-day working to the Chief Officer of the Fire Brigade. By 1953

A Bedford SB coach used by City of Birmingham Ambulance Service to carry expectant mothers to maternity units in the 1950s.

Left: *The classic 1950s ambulance: a Daimler DC27 of the London County Council with bodywork by Barker.*

Below: *Another LCC Daimler, this one with a Hooper body. The differences are a single rather than a double line at waist level and a full-length door for the driver and attendant. LLA 222 was the highest-numbered Daimler in the LCC fleet and was a replacement for a written-off vehicle.*

the Birmingham Fire and Ambulance Service had over a hundred ambulances, including a small number for Civil Defence purposes. The fleet included eight Humber Pullmans, six Daimler DC27s, twenty Austin Sheerlines, twenty Austin Welfarers, thirteen Commers and ten Morris Commercials. 262 full-time staff were employed including ten leading drivers, 158 drivers and attendants, twelve midwives and thirteen ambulance cleaners. There was also a Bedford SB coach which was used to carry expectant mothers for prenatal treatment at Marston Green Hospital on the eastern boundary of the city. Women were given a ticket either by their doctor or the hospital and notified of the time of the coach. Thus Birmingham had a remarkably efficient and effective ambulance service which at least attempted to take account of patient needs and requirements. The ambulance livery of the Birmingham Fire and Ambulance Service was cream with a red waist line.

DAIMLER DC27

Daimler produced the first major special ambulance chassis after the war, in 1949. After considerable research, the classic Daimler DC27 was designed with the needs of London in mind and 120 were initially ordered by the London County Council. The chassis was constructed as low as possible to assist crews with handling stretchers. The first bodies were built by Barker & Company (coachbuilders) and were constructed of ash. The body had a good working head-room and offered a smooth and luxurious ride with excellent stability. The only draw-backs were the absence of a door into the cab area, which restricted communication between crew members, high petrol con-sumption (8.5 miles per gallon on accident work) and questionable brakes, which re-sulted in several spectacular accidents.

The Daimler DC27 became the classic ambulance of the 1950s, but the cost of a bespoke ambulance was relatively high, so that sales were not as great as Daimler might have hoped, although London did standardise on the model. Other users in-cluded Belfast, Birmingham, Carmarthen-shire, Croydon, Cumberland, Hertford-shire, Isle of Wight, Nottingham, Ply-mouth, Salford and Surrey.

Bodies were initially by Barker but some vehicles had bodies by Hooper. The main difference was that Barker bodies had two waist bands whereas the Hooper had only one. The Daimler DC27 continued in serv-ice into the 1960s and a number have been preserved including the first London vehi-cle, fleet number A1 (registration JXP 63).

OTHER VEHICLES

The eighth edition (1961) of *The Brit-ish Commercial Vehicle Industry* listed a variety of models including the Apple-yard (of Leeds) Mark III ambulance mounted on a Morris Commercial LD4 chassis, supplied to the City of Leeds Ambulance Service. The integral Dennis AV Series ambulance, with a flexibly mounted (to reduce vibration from the chassis to the patient) 4 litre engine, was used by numerous municipalities. The Karrier had a body specially designed for their standard chassis (used by Durham County Ambulance Service). Levers Garages Ltd produced three standard styles of 'Lancastrian' body used on the Bedford J1 and CAZ chassis. Herbert Lomas of Wilmslow, Cheshire, claimed that their ambulance bodies could be fit-ted on every type of suitable chassis, in-cluding the Bedford J1 (supplied to Warwickshire County Council) and the Bedford J (as used by the County of Leicester Ambulance Service) as well as the smaller Bedford CA. Wadhams pro-duced composite coachwork designed for use on the Morris J2, LD and FG chassis as well as introducing coachwork of struc-tural plastics for the Morris LD and FG chassis. The use of structural plastics proved a success as it minimised cleaning

A preserved BMC/ Wadhams ambulance in the Shrop-shire Ambulance Service livery of cream with caramel-yellow roof and lining.

A Bedford J1 of the City of Birmingham Ambulance Service. The Bedford formed the backbone of many county and municipal services in the late 1950s and 1960s.

and maintenance as well as reducing re-painting costs. Other firms offering ambulances were Marshall Motor Bodies, Pilchers, Sparshatts and Spurling, mostly aimed at the specialist market. Perhaps less well-known was the firm of Martin Walter Ltd of Folkestone, which produced ambulance bodies for the Bedford Utilicon and J1 as well as a conversion kit for the Vauxhall Victor estate car, which was promoted as a high-speed transfer ambulance.

LIVERIES

The liveries of the services were varied and by no means all used white or cream as the main colour. Croydon and the Isle of Wight used attractive and unusual two-tone grey schemes; Nottingham used Cambridge blue and dove grey; Cambridge and the Isle of Ely Ambulance Service

Not all ambulances were white; here is a Croydon Ambulance Service Humber in two-tone grey on an emergency call in the late 1950s. The Croydon fleet was amalgamated into the London Ambulance Service in the reorganisation of 1965.

vehicles were blue; Salford used the same green as their buses; Bolton's were light grey and Somerset ambulances were dark blue. However, the introduction of plastic and fibreglass bodies saw a gradual move towards basic white and cream schemes.

LONDON GOVERNMENT ACT 1965

When the Greater London Council (GLC) was created in 1965, one ambulance service for the capital was formed from parts of nine existing services, creating the largest ambulance service in the world. The services involved were LCC, Middlesex, the Croydon, East Ham and West Ham County Borough services and parts of Surrey, Essex, Kent and Hertfordshire. On the vehicles the GLC coat of arms replaced the LCC shield. Vehicles taken over initially ran in their old colours but with new markings. Non-standard models, such as Commers previously used by the Croydon service, were soon disposed of.

DENNIS FD4

The Millar Report of 1967 recommended standards of training for ambulance personnel and for the equipment that should be carried on an ambulance.

This report was the foundation of the present-day service. The National Research Development Corporation (NRDC) sponsored research by design consultants, Ogle Research, into the feasibility of producing an efficient emergency ambulance based on the report's recommendations. Within only two years Dennis produced the FD4. Two prototypes were built with front-wheel drive, Jaguar engine, a special low-floor chassis and heavy metal bodies, though fibreglass was intended in production. The first prototype was retained as a test vehicle and may have served as a works ambulance. The second was displayed at the 1968 Commercial Motor Show in the livery of Surrey Ambulance Service. It was evaluated by Surrey and carried fleet number 35, registration WPG 174G. A third vehicle was delivered for trial to Rutland Ambulance Service but was soon written off in an accident with a bus.

The ambulance cost around £3000, which was significantly higher than those based on commercially available chassis. There were no orders, the project was curtailed and the Surrey vehicle was sold at auction. The Dennis test machine was donated to the Kingston upon Thames

A Morris LD/ Wadhams ambulance of Cambridgeshire and the Isle of Ely County Council in an attractive light blue livery, 1960s.

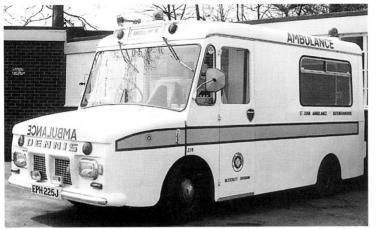

Left: *An attempt at a custom-built ambulance. This is the prototype of the Dennis FD4, built in response to the Millar Report and displayed at the Commercial Motor Show in 1968. Here EPH 225J is shown in the markings of St John Buckinghamshire.*

Right: *Another attempt was the Reeve Sovam of 1973. The prototype was ordered from the drawing board by the LCC. Registered MMF 447L, it was the only one built. It is not clear how much service it saw but it now forms part of the LCC historic fleet.*

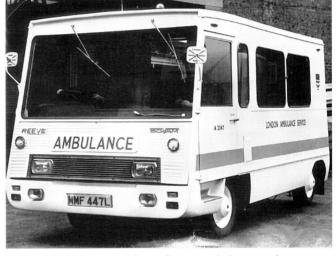

Division of St John Ambulance (the last to provide an agency emergency service to the London Ambulance Service) with registration number EPH 225J. The agency finally ceased in 1975. However, because the non-standard vehicle was expensive to maintain it was sold to St John, Bletchley, Buckinghamshire.

REEVE SOVAM 'CONCORD'

In 1971 Reeve Coachbuilders took over the ambulance side of Smith-Appleyard of Gateshead and a project to build a vehicle based on a chassis by the French company Sovam; the chassis incorporated many of the features recommended in the Millar Report. The London Ambulance Service ordered the prototype, a futuristic-looking vehicle registered MMF 447L, which was delivered in January 1973. No more were ordered but the prototype has been preserved. In the cases of both Dennis

and Reeve Sovam, ambulance services were more concerned about balancing their books than obtaining an ideal ambulance.

MILITARY AMBULANCES OF THE POST-WAR PERIOD

The Austin four-by-four 1 ton ambulance was developed to meet an Air Ministry requirement for crash rescue operations at airfields. The vehicle could carry four stretcher cases. Bodywork was by Mann Egerton Ltd of Norwich and Mickleover Transport Company of Park Royal, London.

A chassis was developed by Ford to meet the General Service (GS) requirement for a four-wheel-drive 3 ton vehicle. The body was designed to accommodate four stret-

This post-war military ambulance is a Bedford CF of the Royal Naval Hospital Haslar, with bodywork by Herbert Lomas. Although people think of ambulances as carrying red crosses, it was only those belonging to the armed forces or the British Red Cross Society that displayed them after the Second World War. This vehicle was photographed at St Thomas's Hospital, London, in 1988.

An Army 1 tonne Land-Rover ambulance. Blue beacons and repeaters, two-tone sirens and green and white chequered linings, as used during the long ambulance dispute of 1989-90, have been added. The Westminster Hospital, London, where this photograph was taken, has now closed.

A Land-Rover Series II military ambulance in service with the Territorial Army in 1989.

chers and was produced by Spurling Motor Bodies Ltd of Dagenham, Mulliners Ltd of Birmingham and Duple Motor Bodies of Hendon.

However, the mainstay of post-war military ambulances in the United Kingdom has been the Land-Rover. The first purpose-built Land-Rover ambulances were on Series I 107 chassis dating from late 1954. In one respect this early vehicle was better than the later Series II and III vehicles as it had higher headroom in the rear compartment. For the 109 Series II in 1958 Wadham Stringer produced batch conversions for a small Royal Navy ambulance contract and in 1960 Mickleover Transport Company and Marshalls of Cambridge were building a dedicated military ambulance to an official specification that set the standard for British military ambulances for over fifteen years. These and the improved Series IIA ambulances saw service with the Army, the Royal Navy and the RAF, who used them both as airfield crash vehicles and for mountain rescue. Their long service and subsequent further use by civilian operations resulted from the amazingly low mileages recorded, especially on airfields.

The 101 1 tonne forward-control Land-Rover appeared in 1975, with a perma-

nent four-wheel-drive system using the power train from the Range Rover; ambulances constructed by Marshalls of Cambridge entered service in 1976. The red cross symbols were carried on hinged flaps which could be opened to display the crosses or lowered to cover them when the large white square might detract from the vehicle's camouflage.

On civilian emergency use during the long civilian ambulance dispute of 1989-90 military ambulances carried additional green and white check markings, extra blue beacons and front repeaters and sirens to make them more visible in winter weather conditions.

The Land Rover 127 of 1987, bodied by Marshalls of Cambridge, had a window on only the driver's side of the rear compartment. Used by all three services, this model went to the Gulf War and to Bosnia. In the Gulf it carried an attractive two-tone camouflage with both red cross and red crescent markings.

Since the 1970s civilian-type ambulances, mainly based on the Bedford CF and Ford Transit, have been used to support military hospitals. Most are white with red crosses and they normally carry civilian registrations. Navy Range Rover ambulances at Fleet Air Arm stations are bright yellow.

29

MODERN CIVILIAN AMBULANCES

Ambulance services continued to develop and expand until 1974 when responsibility for ambulance services in England and Wales was transferred to area health authorities. The number of services was reduced from 120 to forty, causing problems for the new bodies set up to manage the services. The variety and type of ambulances which came into the ownership of the area health authorities was immense and some form of standardisation was essential as well as desirable.

Another benefit was the noticeable updating of fleets. By the early 1980s most ambulance services were operating vehicles no more than six years old on frontline emergency work. These were mainly based on either the Ford Transit or the Bedford CF light commercial chassis with bodywork provided by a variety of bodybuilders including Wadham Stringer of Waterlooville, Hampshire, Pilcher Greene of Burgess Hill, West Sussex, N. Hanlon Ltd of Longford, Ireland, Steerdrive of Macclesfield, Cheshire, and Mountain Range of Crewe, Cheshire. London used Bedford CFs with bodywork by Dormobile.

In 1986 the specialist role performed by the ambulance service was recognised by the award of the Ambulance Service Shield, which quickly became known as the 'crown badge'. The badge soon became the standard marking on ambulances, each county including its title in the wording on the shield.

In the 1990s specialised paramedical skills are highly emphasised and response performance targets are published. Rapid-response units ranging from motorcycles (West Midlands, London, Avon, Sussex and Scotland) and cars to specialised vehicles (such as the Renault Espace in London) have been evaluated and helicopter ambulances are being operated both in rural areas where distances are great and in urban areas where heavy traffic may delay road vehicles, for example the Helicopter Emergency Medical Service in London.

High-visibility colour schemes have been adopted for emergency and accident work, and often more restrained liveries on other vehicles used for out-patient transport. Some services use the blue 'Star of Life' badge in addition to the crown badge.

Ambulances from overseas have been introduced, for example Mercedes, Renault, Peugeot Talbot, GMC and Chevrolet, perhaps because fewer British firms are in the market. Those that are include Customline of Brighouse, West Yorkshire, with their Lazer models using Ford Transit, Iveco Ford, Leyland DAF and Mercedes chassis; and Iveco Ford, who promote their 40-10 and 45-10 High Roof Turbo Dailys as front-line ambulances, recommending bodywork by Taurus Bodies of Stockport and the Premia body by the UVG (Universal Vehicle Group) Ltd using the Ford Transit chassis.

The Ambulance Service crown badge. This is from a Wiltshire vehicle. The only difference between services is the county name on the shield.